Robert Morris Copeland

The Most Beautiful City in America

Essay and plan for the improvement of the city of Boston

Robert Morris Copeland

The Most Beautiful City in America
Essay and plan for the improvement of the city of Boston

ISBN/EAN: 9783337419783

Printed in Europe, USA, Canada, Australia, Japan

Cover: Foto ©Andreas Hilbeck / pixelio.de

More available books at **www.hansebooks.com**

The Most Beautiful City in America.

ESSAY AND PLAN

FOR

THE IMPROVEMENT

OF THE

CITY OF BOSTON.

BY

ROBERT MORRIS COPELAND.

BOSTON:
LEE & SHEPARD.
1872.

THIS ESSAY AND PLAN

FOR THE IMPROVEMENT OF THE CITY IS RESPECTFULLY OFFERED TO THE
CONSIDERATION OF BOSTONIANS, BY ONE WHO, WHEREVER HE
MAY BE TAKEN BY NECESSITY, BUSINESS, OR PLEASURE,
WILL ALWAYS REMEMBER THE BEAUTY OF HIS
BIRTHPLACE, AND WHO,
HOWEVER MUCH HE MAY ADMIRE THE ENTERPRISE AND PROGRESS OF
OTHER CITIES, BELIEVES THAT BOSTON MAY BE MADE THE
MOST CONVENIENT, AS WELL AS THE MOST
BEAUTIFUL CITY IN AMERICA.

THE importance to a city of sufficient room in its streets to transport all the freight and merchandise which comes by cars or vessels, cannot be over-estimated. Boston is using every effort to enlarge her business, although, even now, a balky horse or an overturned coal-cart, in one of her narrow streets, can arrest the business of the city until the obstruction is removed; and by that delay cause men to break important engagements, travellers to lose the cars or steamboats, and create general inconvenience for the whole business community. Last summer, it is said that fifteen miles of freight cars were waiting at one time to be unloaded, and this winter our railroads have been obliged to refuse or hold back western freight because of our inability to handle and store it. These facts cannot be ignored; and if the city is too small or inconvenient for the present business, what will she do with the increase that must follow new railroads and canals, and new investments of energy and capital?

Mathematics teach us that what is true of a part of any body is true of its whole; and this we can apply to the domestic and business wants of a growing city, as well as to men's private affairs. If a farmer's barn cannot hold his crops he builds larger and better. Manufacturers extend their mills and warehouses to meet the increasing demands of their business. Merchants plan roads and railroads, build wharves and ships, and try in all legitimate ways to increase their opportunities for doing business. When one's house becomes too small or inconvenient for his growing family, or improving fortunes, he either adds to the dwelling, or sells and builds better. All these progressive movements are in a sense compulsory and costly, and very few persons ever complete any such undertaking without learning how much more they want than they supposed at the outset, and finding that the necessary changes and improvements cost more than was at first expected. This well-known fact that follows every kind of improvement should teach the citizens of a growing city the importance of trying to foresee the city's future necessities, and to arrange its systems of public improvements so that all possible wants might be properly provided for without unnecessary cost, or the disarrangement of existing rights of property and business. If it is a serious inconvenience to a man's family to have his house raised or moved, or enlarged, it is proportionally a greater trouble to the inhabitants of a district, when their streets must be ripped up for sewers, water, or gas; or, to alter the general grade, their houses must all be screwed up into the air, or be lowered by taking out the foundation, or be cut into pieces to open a new street. If it is a tax on the merchant or manufacturer to build railroads, wharves, warehouses, and machine shops, but a tax borne because of the reward to follow, it is no less a tax on the income of every man, however poor, when a city must alter its series of drains, grades, sewers, open new streets, remove obstructing buildings, and cut down venerable trees, to give more room, better drainage, more light and air, or improve the chances of travel.

Private individuals are excusable for not laying very wide and deep foundations for their business, because it requires a great expenditure of capital, which the prudent man dislikes to risk until his business is assured; and when its profits are sure, it is often too late to improve or extend his facilities without loss in money, or time, or by interruption of the daily progress of his work. When any particular kind of business is well understood, and the laws of supply and demand which regulate it are thoroughly comprehended, individuals, or corporations, do dare to plan largely and grandly, to make sure that as their business increases, the means of doing it may respond; but, generally, successful enterprises grow from very small beginnings, and much more slowly than they would if not cramped by the narrow limits imposed at the outset.

All this, which is true of every individual enterprise, is still more true when applied to the public life and wants of a city. (A city is a warehouse for the collection and distribution of the products which contribute to the luxuries or necessities of life;) and as a village always grows up around a manufactory, because the mill must have operatives, and operatives houses, so the town, or city, grows in numbers because many persons must be employed to buy and sell, collect and distribute the merchandise that rolls in over the railroads, comes down the river, or is landed on its wharves.

There are some cities, like Philadelphia, Manchester, Birmingham, etc., which are devoted mostly to manufactures, and are producing, rather than collecting and distributing points; but most cities collect and distribute more than they make. The wealth of a city depends upon the amount of business done; and accordingly its merchants try, by building railroads and steamships, to divert to particular points all the merchandise which moves over the country.

Boston early aided in building railroads, and Massachusetts is covered with a network of iron rails, and is seeking a new inlet and outlet by going through the solid hills. We used to build or own ships, and there have been times when Boston ships rivalled in number and enterprise any other city in the world. Whatever is the cause of the decline in shipping we are alive to its decay, and every year new plans are formed and furthered to increase our commerce. Supposing that all the new plans and combinations are successful, what next? We must, like the farmer, the manufacturer, the householder, build anew. We must have new wharves, larger and more convenient warehouses, better means of access by road and steam to all parts of the city, better dwellings for rich and poor. This is as obvious, or certain to be the necessity, if our business increases, as that the bucket which holds but one gallon cannot hold two. When we have the business, when the far-reaching plans of the board of trade and the railroad manager quadruples the stream of merchandise which flows in and out of this city, where shall we find the conveniences for doing our business? With more merchandise must come the many people who handle it, who own it, and who can supply the domestic wants of the population, who congregate wherever population is increasing, combined with those who like to live in that city which is most convenient and best supplied with the luxuries and necessities of life. But people and business, merchandise and houses, whilst they mark the growth and importance of a city, carry with them other necessities which in a short time force themselves into notice and require to be cared for. With a more dense population, contagious disease increases, crime becomes more frequent, amusement and pleasures must be provided.

With people comes waste; sewerage flows from countless drains carrying disease in its current, — sewerage which may be a servant or a master. As a servant, it may help to beautify the country or feed its population; as a master, it kills all it touches. For an increasing population there must be houses; with new houses comes the increased danger of fire, which may sweep over the city, destroying vast amounts of property and life. These are present dangers; not chimeras, but pressing impending possibilities, only to be postponed or checked by forethought and increasing vigilance. If all the dangers are foreseen and provided for, there is still the acknowledged want of amusement; all work and no play makes Jack not only a dull boy, but a sodden, dangerous fellow, whose natural instincts will sometimes break loose and do even greater mischief to others than to himself.

How are we providing for these necessities, danger, and pleasures in this city, which spreads out about our beautiful bay, and into whose embrace we are inviting the business of the world? Remembering that what is true of a part is true of the whole, and that with every added mile of railroad, thousand tons of freight, or new factory, there must come more people, more houses, more danger of fire and disease, more necessity for amusement; what are the boards of trade, the railroad managers, the city fathers, doing to entertain the army of visitors, the increasing number of inhabitants, to reduce the danger of conflagration, to check the possible progress of disease, to make the city a beautiful, as well as a convenient home to live in?

These questions and the considerations which flow from them are quite as important now, and require as much deliberation and planning as how to get through the Hoosac mountains, or to divert the grain of the west from New York or Portland, to our wharves and warehouses.

What does the sagacious business man, whether farmer, householder, merchant, or manufacturer, do with the property he controls, when about to start a new or enlarge an old business? He looks at the ends in view, and tries to adapt his means to them. If he is to erect buildings, he carefully considers their uses, sees how much surface they must cover, how they can be made most accessible and convenient to each other, and tries to give each one a suitable position. If by want of skill or knowledge the barn occupies the place where the house should have been, if the store is too near the fac-

2

tory, if the drainage will not run away from the buildings, if there is wasted room, the work must all be changed hereafter, with added cost, and loss of time. This is equally true of the city. Why, if men can plan a palace, a church, a capital, a city hall, a school-house, a manufactory, a depot, a railroad, so that they shall be each year more and more convenient for their intended uses, should they be unable to plan for the entire domestic and internal arrangements and conveniences of a group of such buildings, and the adjoining dwellings, stores, and domestic conveniences which are necessary for the population which is to use them?

POSSIBLE TO MAKE A PLAN FOR LAYING OUT A CITY.

If the group can be planned for, why not the town or city? If Boston has a present area of a definite number of square miles, with its destiny plainly marked out as a commercial and manufacturing city, why should the city's progress be haphazard and halting, sometimes making one, sometimes another advance with no apparent relation to each other, or the future improvements which must be required? How best to use Boston's area must be a problem which admits of division into parts, of discussion and measurement, and a plan can be as well digested for its future progress so as to do full justice to the wants of a future population as for the laying out and construction of a building for public or domestic use.

The sole difference, or hindrance to such planning is, that we have not been accustomed to plan in this way. We have supposed that, for some unnamed reason, planning for a city's growth and progress could only be done as it grows; that no one can foresee sufficiently the future requirements of business to wisely provide for them. This is a fallacious belief. It often happens as time passes that some line of railroad does not wholly meet the wants of the country it traverses. Some unnoticed waterfall, some local advantage, or personal preference, or energy, may start a town into size and value which was a swamp or pasture when the railroad was first constructed and which may in its day of prosperity demand new facilities. But whilst this possibility exists, it is no less true that the line of any railroad will gradually become thickly settled, if not wholly convenient at first. Men will bring their factories and dwellings near the great feeder, and adapt their wants to the circumstances of the case.

The city whose area is carefully studied, which shows by plan where wharves may be built, where new avenues are to be laid out, and where factories may congregate; where parks, gardens, and palaces, if desired, may be made, will grow in a sure, orderly, and progressive way, and as it grows have all the central vigor of the great railroad or manufactory; merchandise can be easily transported, business done, water and gas supplied, amusements furnished, fires limited, and sewage provided for.

When a man or company wish to begin a new or a valuable business, they can adapt their wants to the city plan. If they own land in the domestic part of the city they will exchange it for a site in the business or manufacturing part, and no one's rights be infringed.

It seems, at first, as if such planning for the future use of the landed estate of a city would be an interference with the rights of private property. But it is certainly less of a hardship or infringement on private right to point out how, in future, land may be used for the best good of the whole, than when the necessity comes to drive an avenue through a man's factory, close up his business by indicting it as a nuisance, cut down the road in front of his house, leaving him to get down as best he may, or raise his house into the air

to be got into only by a ladder. Not only is forethought less
of an outrage, but it costs far less to the corporation and to
the citizens who make the corporation, than after-thought.

If these general propositions are correct, they may be
divided and applied to Boston, and their value tested by their
local application. In order to make my ideas plain, I have
made a general plan for the street and public grounds of
Boston, which may be found at the end of this pamphlet, and
to which I invite the reader's attention. A city or town is
to be considered as a whole, and in relation to all of its wants,
as well as its necessities; and firstly, its business must be
amply provided for. As commerce, whether by land or sea,
increases, many kinds of domestic manufacture must increase
to supply the wants of the trading community, and as one
kind of business is sure to bring another, all the suitable
area for business should be set aside for that purpose.

WATER FRONT.

Commerce will require the water-front and a connection
with the railroads that bring and take away merchandise.
The land bounding the water-front will be naturally more
level than that farther inland, and better for roads and heavy
warehouses. The whole water-front of Boston therefore
should be connected by a broad and well made avenue open
to teams and cars.

This avenue need not, and should not, directly bound the
water, as the shore is most valuable for wharves, landings and
stores; but it should approach so near that it would give the
amplest means of access and departure, and connect with
the water all the great depots and manufacturing parts of
the town, either by direct contact, or by radial and broad
avenues, which should cross the level parts of the city, or
follow up the lines of valleys and the sides of streams.
Where all the land is level like Philadelphia, or Chicago,

the avenue of connection need not be confined into what we here should call the natural directions, because a level city can be made as accessible in one direction as in another; but in Boston, as heavy freight demands easy grades, the natural line must be followed. Our great radial connecting avenues would leave the broad Marginal avenue by the bridges as now, by the Western, by Dorchester avenue and the interior avenues, Tremont street, Washington street and Shawmut avenue; but these interior avenues should be united by a cross street of equal width, and dignity with the Marginal avenue which could start from the eastern end of Summer street, and gradually curve through Essex to Boylston, or to Pleasant, and through Boylston, or Pleasant, and Charles between the Common and Public Garden to the connection of the Western and Marginal avenue. On this street and its connecting avenue 100 feet wide, which would circle the State House, there should be a freight railroad and as the grade would be easy, with no hills to ascend and descend, and no crowded streets to impede locomotion, loaded teams could pass more rapidly from the Providence to the Fitchburg depots, than by the more direct route through Tremont, Sudbury or Washington street, Dock and Haymarket Squares. All the net work of streets within this circle could be devoted to the retail trade, law, dwellings, etc.; along this avenue there would be plenty of room for all the great warehouses of the city engaged in receiving and forwarding goods by rail or water, and the best facilities for loading and unloading. This arrangement would not require a very costly or radical change, as it could be made by widening already existing streets, with a few trifling exceptions. As soon as the avenue gave expansion and freedom to traffic the tendency of all wholesale business would be to withdraw from the narrow and crooked streets of old Boston, leaving them in whole or part to be re-converted into dwellings where either poor or rich men might find convenient city homes near all the depots, the crossing lines of horse cars, and the common. The hills which are such obstacles to heavy locomotion would be, as they used to be, the most desirable places for residences ; for they give good drainage, good circulation of air, and many of them fine views of the harbor and the country.

Starting from the girdling and parent avenue, radial lines would cross the bridges and ferries to East Boston, Charlestown, Somerville and Cambridge. These cities, with their extensive water fronts ought to be included in our general plan, and their local advantages for commerce, etc., be utilized and provided for.

This, however, must be neglected or omitted in this essay, for we can only properly dispose of what we have, however desirable it may be that we should have more, and it is obvious that the same reasoning and system which applies to old Boston would also apply to any towns to be annexed.

To return to the junction of Western avenue: This street, as long as it remains in the boundaries of the city, clings to the Charles river on one side, and bounds the yet unimproved Back Bay lands. The Back Bay having been selected as the situation for our best dwellings, it would be agreeable to their owners to devote this water-front to some ornamental use. But the city cannot afford to give up any of her internal deep water to ornament, for the time will come in spite of the trouble of bridges and draws, when every foot of the Charles river bank will be wanted for yards and wharves to supply by water the population south west of Boston with coarse articles of freight, or will be important for the factories which must have a water-front, as well as a connection with streets and railroads. If there were no fine houses on the Back Bay the whole of the level area between Charles river and South Cove should be laid out for stores and factories. Here the land is level, easy of access, and convenient to the railroads and the water. But if devoted to commerce and business, even more than when covered with costly houses, it would be necessary to reserve large spaces for public grounds, in order to prevent population from becoming too dense, and to serve as a barrier to the sweep of a great fire. Such central commons would connect with the common and public garden, and should be combined with the yet unfilled Back Bay and Parker's hill into a general system, so as to become practically one great park. The largest part of the yet unfilled marshes should be reserved for public uses, and treated as will be hereafter described.

RADIAL AVENUES TO BROOKLINE AND ROXBURY.

Leaving the Western, and returning along the Marginal avenue, we shall cross several of the great exits from the city — Boylston street, Columbus avenue, Tremont street, Shawmut avenue, Washington street, and Harrison avenue. Let us follow them out to Roxbury. They and their connections traverse a level country until we get fairly into the Roxbury Main avenue. Parkers street, Columbus avenue, and the parallel avenues and Tremont street should be gathered into one large square near the present Providence depot; business and travel centering here would then diverge by Washington street to Brookline and Roxbury, and following the valley of Stony Brook up Pynchon street to Centre and Codman streets, where it might again divide and pass by those two streets to West Roxbury. The line of business should stop at Washington street, all the breweries, and factories be cleared away, and Stony Brook from its entrance into Boston be purified of sewerage and restored to its pristine beauty. Its banks rising on one side to Parker's hill, on the other to the Highlands, would give the finest

sites for a good class of houses; in fact along these hill-
sides palaces might be built which would be worthy of the
situation. No other city and no other part of Boston can
surpass the building sites which could be selected between
Parker's hill and Warren street in Roxbury. No factories
should ever come into this picturesque region. The grades,
which are too steep for heavy loads, only make a pleasant
diversity of surface for light wagons and driving; and if
selections were to be made for public grounds this part of
the city would grow every day more and more valuable for
building purposes. Family mansions would cover the hill-
sides which would become endeared to generations and
acquire a dignity with time.

On this side of the city there should be large reservations
for the public, and here, as everywhere else in Boston, we
should improve the wonderful advantages the rocky hills
offer, both by their local beauty and by the views they open
of the distant landscape of bay, river, and mountain. Parker's Hill, the old fort, and Simmons woods on the Highlands, the old Chemical Works, the city almshouse, and
the valley of Stony Brook, and part of the old Codman
place should be treated as a park. Not all the land to be
reserved, but only small groups of buildings to be permitted,
and those mostly of a public character.

NEW SITE FOR CITY BUILDINGS. — PUTNAM SQUARE·

Sites in these reservations could be selected for charitable
and public institutions, and a large common should be made
near the Norfolk House and Dr. Putnam's church, to be surrounded by the city and State buildings of the future. Here
where there is plenty of room, where a fine building could
be seen and appreciated, we should build such a city hall
and State-house as would be worthy of the greatness of

Boston. As the city grows and the demand for room in the
public offices increases, and as courts overrun their limits,
the narrow streets and steep hill-sides of old Boston will
become more and more inconvenient; here is the great situation for a group of edifices which shall meet and satisfy every
want, as it is central to the city and easily approached on all
sides. From Putuam Square following Dudley or Washington street, we strike Shawmut avenue and Washington
street as it leaves Boston Neck. These two great streets
should be combined with Harrison avenue near the present
City Hotel and Guild's block into one great plaza.

ROXBURY SQUARE.

Five or six acres to be called Roxbury square could be
cleared of buildings at this point, and become one open
square, to be planted and decorated in the future with foun-
tains and statuary, but to be the central point from which
other avenues may start. This square should mark the
limit of business other than the retail trade. In fact, Shawmut avenue and Warren street, with its branches, Walnut
street and Grove Hall avenue, give no land suitable for
business purposes, but beautiful situations for dwellings of
all kinds. A great population could be accommodated in
this area, and a tract of twenty to fifty acres should be taken
out of the land now owned by the Williams family, Mr.
Harris, and others, connecting Grove Hall in Dorchester with
the Codman estate, the Highlands, and Parker's hill, in Roxbury. This land should not be taken of uniform width or
shape, but of such a shape as would give the largest amount of
frontage for houses, and would make a link in the beautiful
drive to be made from Savin hill through a park-like country
to Brookline, or by the Parker's hill, park, and Common-
wealth avenue to the common in the old city.

2

Returning to Roxbury square we find that there is a large area bounded by Pleasant, Dudley, and Houghton streets, and Meeting-house hill on the one side, and the South cove on the other, which is reasonably level and has the double advantage of a water-front and railroad facilities. Here, again, business, commerce and manufactures may increase enormously before the available space would be used up, and this land is of easy access to all parts of the city.

DORCHESTER AVENUE.

The great marginal, or Boston avenue, which we left at the corner or foot of Summer street, should follow the shore line on or near Dorchester avenue to Glover's corner, where a broad branch should turn by Commercial street through Commercial point to Port Norfolk.

Returning to Glover's corner, the avenue should continue to Field's corner, where it could again divide into two parts, one following Adams street to near Neponset, where it should bend along the line of the Neponset river up to Milton Lower Mills to rejoin there the main avenue continued from Field's corner.

In this region lying between the great Boston, or Dorchester avenue and the Neponset river, and the water, there are several hills which would be of little use for business purposes, but very valuable for the public; their tops should be reserved and laid out as little parks, and their sides be devoted to dwellings, whilst the valleys on each side would come into the general system as business area. This extensive region, stretching from the Old Colony depot, in Boston, to Milton Lower Mills, is well adapted to many kinds of commercial, and to any manufacturing uses, is easily drained, and if the hills were reserved for public grounds could never be ravaged by any great fire, for the hills would present a barrier that would give time to stop a fire or to change its direction.

WATER FRONT OF DORCHESTER AND ROXBURY FOR BUSINESS.

On this side of Boston there are many very advantageous places for special manufactures. The line of Neponset river, or the valleys of the streams which empty into the bay at Harrison square, and the river at Neponset, are very well suited to the breweries which now deface the valley of Stony Brook and the flanks of Parker's hill. The Neponset river and these large brooks give plenty of water; the hills which make their banks, cellar room for any amount of storage; and there is tide-water near by to bring and take the heavy freight that brewers have to handle. If ever the water-fronts and the spaces already assigned to the business of the city prove too small, the valleys of the streams which empty at Harrison square and Neponset, offer a large and tolerably level country, well adapted to any heavy manufacturing business, and of a character to permit a large operative population to cluster about the workshops. As population and business spread, the principle of reserving all the hill-tops for public grounds should be rigidly adhered to, which, as is shown on the map, would dot this whole region with little parks, which would be a present and enduring source of pleasure to that class of population who have neither time nor means to take them to much more beautiful places if they are distant. Each of these parklets would gather about it good houses, the residences of wealthy, or well-to-do men, who would feel encouraged to build well and decorate their estates, and thus we should still further insure the beauty, health, and security of the city against disease and fire; for the larger and better the houses, the more sure to be well drained, and to be attended or surrounded with gardens and trees. In passing from one part of the city to another, a stranger would never be out of sight of the beauties of nature, and the apparent inconveniences of the city for business and for a dense population, would, without injuring any domestic economy, continue to be, as now, its greatest beauty and its chief attractive charm.

ROXBURY SQUARE AND GROVE HALL.

Let us now return to Roxbury square and begin our journey anew, — following Warren street, which, as the continuation of Harrison avenue, should be one of the broad streets of the future city, up to its junction with Grove Hall avenue. To that point the land on each side is good for building purposes ; and although we must mourn the destruction of the beautiful May's woods, there is a great and good variety of surface.

This region has become a favorite one with horticulturists, and the street is lined with greenhouses. As population increases, land will become too valuable for such uses ; but until then this situation is certainly well adapted for that kind of business, but it should never be allowed to be devoted to purely business purposes.

At Grove Hall, Warren street is lost in Blue Hill avenue and Washington street. Let us follow the latter to Milton Lower Mills. We traversed a very hilly and broken country ; a ridge rising between the lower Dorchester lands, which we give up to business, and some broad and rolling farms on the south, which can be used in several ways.

This part of Dorchester is worthy of close study, because as yet, it is but slightly improved by costly buildings, and therefore is a part of the city whose future can be decided with less expense than the more thickly-settled parts.

NEPONSET RIVER.

In this busy country, every stream, even if of small volume, will be brought into some use as an aid to manufacturers, and we find that the Neponset river is no exception to the general rule. Taking the two villages of Mattapan and the Lower Mills as nuclei of manufacturing villages, we may expect that the line of the stream will be used in many ways which are connected with the manufacturing interests already established, and in the progress of time population will become more dense about these two villages, and will spread back into the land which lies between the Warren and Grove Hall avenues. A good deal of this land is low and marshy, and nearly level, being the basin of the Neponset river, but it would permit a dense population to collect. It cannot be doubted that nearly level land, easily traversed by horse and steam cars, and by wagons and carts of those who transport all articles of domestic use, is best suited to men of moderate mean, and Boston has in this part of her boundary room for a very large poor population. Crossed by the Milton railroad, by the Hartford and Erie, and about to be tapped by a branch of the Old Colony, it will be sure to become thickly settled. Here, for two reasons, we should reserve a large space for public improvements; firstly, because the population of the future will need and enjoy the reservation; secondly, because the land is reasonably cheap now, and by and by will be very costly.

Both large and small parks should be near the most thickly settled parts of a town, and if a space is selected any where in Boston, proper care should be taken to plan for the future growth of population in its vicinity. If it is possible to provide by restrictions, or regulations, for the erection of cheap and comfortable houses near the chosen land for the poorer classes, the great purpose of the park would be more certainly secured. In order to unite the Mattapan district with the rest of our public system, the Marginal, or Boston avenue, should continue along the Neponset, from Milton Lower Mills, following River street through Mattapan to our southern boundary. At Mattapan, Boston avenue should turn on Blue Hill avenue, to Grove Hall, and then through the Williams, Harris, and Otis estates, as is shown by the plan, and keep through that park by a continuous and easy line to Brookline and the Western avenue.

This plan for laying out the south side of Boston, and to mark the boundaries of the business, the population, and the public grounds of the city may be left here.

SAVIN HILL AND SOUTH BOSTON.

Let us turn along Dorchester or Boston avenue to the city, crossing a large extent of marshes which at low tide are mud flats, and at high water are a mixture of sedge sea mud and floating sewage. This body of land lying between Savin hill, Roxbury Point and South Boston, offers a field for speculation and business. It has two water fronts and two lines of railroads. Consequently, it is particularly well adapted to commerce and manufactures. As soon as the demand warrants, speculators will raise the flats into good building land, by the aid of the gravel of Dorchester and Quincy, and reserving the South Boston heights as suitable and sacred to good dwellings, we may expect that the entire water-fronts, and the Dorchester Neck will become densely populated with warehouses, and workshops.

On our left as we go towards the city, and on the southern shore of the South Cove, Dorchester brook empties; this brook, the old boundary of Dorchester and Roxbury, is but little better now than a sewer: it flows through a deep valley and ought to be improved. If its basin were cleansed, and dammed at proper points, back of Mount Harrison, north of Stoughton-street crossing, and in the South Cove itself, at least three large and very desirable fresh-water ponds could be made valuable for use and beauty doing for the east what the Parker hill ponds would do for the west side of the city. To return to the Boston, or Dorchester avenue, where it crosses Dorchester street in South Boston, one of the great South Boston connections with the main system can be made. Let the avenue follow Dorchester to 8th, 8th to N, N to P, P to First, and First over Second to Broadway, and Broadway to Albany street, in Boston. Telegraph, Dorchester street and Broadway, should be made wide avenues. This avenue would pass through a large reservation on the northeast side of South Boston, including the grounds of the Insane Asylum.

EAST BOSTON.

Passing through the city across the Chelsea bridge, or the East Boston ferry, we touch Boston's other extremity, and see at once how much it would be for the interest of Chelsea, Charlestown, Somerville, and Cambridge, to be combined with East Boston. But, neglecting for the present all the advantages and disadvantages of annexation, what is the best use to make of this side of the city? East Boston has deep water and can bring to her wharves the heaviest vessels which can enter our harbors; her shores, and the banks of the Mystic river used to be the favorite workshop of the ship builders. The deep water is there, and the vessels can still come to the wharves; but the decline of ship-building has left many a busy yard unoccupied, but business ever presses forward, and new arts and manufacturers will occupy the abandoned space. Here, all the railroads on this side of Boston can easily bring their merchandise, and in time East

Boston for one set of railroads, and South Boston for the other, will become important receiving and distributing points, and the vicinity of the railroads and their workshops, will be given up to purely railroad business.

The wharves and railroads will be followed by warehouses, grain elevators and manufactories of heavy kinds of merchandise. The crowd of attendant laborers, and operatives, will make a dense city, which will cover all the rolling ground and climb the hillsides ; but the hilltops here, as in Dorchester, should be saved for public grounds, and be connected by a broad boulevard with Chelsea beach and the sea at Winthrop. The local character and scenery of East Boston is so unlike that of the south side of Boston that all the public improvements should differ in their treatment, and thus give a great variety to the public interest and beauty of the city. Much as we love and praise the view from Parker's hill, or the many high points in Dorchester, none of them can show the visitor greater variety and beauty of landscape than the crest of the hills in East Boston, and Chelsea.

Before these hills is spread a landscape that one can never tire of looking at, whether he studies the busy shifting of scenes in the harbor always lively with sail and steamer, or watches the breaking line of foam as wave after wave rolls up on Chelsea beach, or gazes inland over the level but ever beautiful marshes of Malden and Medford, with their picturesque outlines and background of hill and forest-clad ledges. In East Boston, as elsewhere, the wants of business should be first considered, and to accommodate the movement of freight there should be a broad avenue, or boulevard, following the deep water to Chelsea.

EAST BOSTON'S WATER FRONT.

One branch of the avenue, more for pleasure than for business, should be extended through Breed's Island and Winthrop to Point Shirley, and return along the shore to Chelsea beach and connect with the Lynn turnpike. This turnpike widened to one hundred feet would give a suitable entrance to the city from the towns west, and if joined by an avenue with Chelsea street in East Boston, would properly connect all the water front, and facilitate the movement of freight which business would require.

Barriers to the progress of fire, and proper ventilation of the city, could be secured by parks on the hill-tops and small squares at the points shown on the plan, the largest one to be made on land yet to be filled, and a reservation on Breed's Island.

Such a system of radiating and connecting avenues will give freedom of movement for business or pleasure in every part of the city, and will develop its natural resources and make its disadvantages of surface useful and ornamental, and leave the city as convenient as if it were a level piece of land, and infinitely more beautiful.

THE BEAUTY OF BOSTON AS IMPORTANT AS ITS ECONOMY.

So far the problem has been discussed with no especial reference to the possible beauty of the city, its beauty being treated as of no consequence, or wholly secondary to its business wants; but when we think of the beauty which every city ought properly to have, and which attends upon all good combinations of irregular surface with buildings and decorative treatment, we see that the arrangement of Boston's territory which is the best for her business, is equally good for beauty; and if a plan similar to the one suggested were adopted, she would become not only a most convenient business city, but also very beautiful. It might be very properly claimed that the beauty of a city is of as much importance to it as its business convenience, and that great sacrifices could be made with propriety if thereby increased beauty could be secured.

Whether we care for it or not, admit it or not, Boston cannot be surpassed in picturesqueness. Its irregularity of surface, its hills and valleys, rocky ledges, wide meadows, fine trees, winding streams, broad harbor, inland bays, make variety and beauty in every direction, and a beauty which still continues to be manifest, in spite of the efforts which have been made to destroy it.

The value and reality of beauty cannot be denied, and although there are men so indifferent to it that they would as soon look at a cabbage as at a rose, at the image before a tobacconist's shop as at the Greek slave, at a flock of garbage ducks paddling in the mud-hole known as the Back Bay as at a wild swan floating in a mountain lake, yet their stolidity and ignorance do not reduce the reality or value of beauty.

Beauty in some form or other is growing to be daily more widely recognized as an important element in every life. Art gardens, schools of design, buildings constructed with closest attention to architectural effect are becoming the pride of our cities; color and form are sought to decorate even the articles which are simply useful in their character; men who give all their lives to the study of effect and the creation of the beautiful in contradistinction to useful things, increase in numbers, and some of them produce works which claim the admiration of the multitude as well as of the few who avow their love for and belief in beauty. Every well-balanced school system offers art-culture of some kind as part of its

curriculum. Can we, then, deny that the actual beauty of
the city we live in is of great consequence, and expose our
rolling surfaces, our hills and streams, and water margins to
the caprice or stupidity of men who deny that beauty is of
any consequence compared with utility?

We have so far discussed our city to see what utility
demands for it; let us look at her now as the future home
of men who love the beautiful, a love which can be developed
and strengthened by its presence in the structure, form, and
details of the homes in which children grow to manhood,
and in the landscape which greets them as they pass through
the city streets, or look abroad from its hill-tops.

PUBLIC GROUNDS USEFUL AS WELL AS BEAUTIFUL.

As we have gone from section to section of the city by
avenue or cross street, we have pointed out spaces to be
reserved for the public, and to be laid out as ornamental
grounds. These places are just so many valuable acres
taken out of the public domain, worth a great deal of money
per acre, and will cost yet more money for decoration and
maintenance. If taken they will have an economical value
for ventilation, and as purifiers of the air of the city, and as
barriers against fire, and as interrupting the spread of contagious disease. The sanitary arguments in their favor are
so numerous that we need give no space to them; but let us
disregard every sanitary or economical argument and discuss
the public grounds of Boston wholly relative to their ornamental value.

Does Boston, as a city, need any public parks or squares
for their ornamental and pleasurable value? To recount all
of the arguments against any outlay for that purpose would
require considerable space, and would be open to the objec-

tion that we did not state all that could be said, or did not give sufficient weight to the objections; therefore, further than is required to bring out the affirmative reasons, no notice will be taken of them. Let us look at Boston and its suburbs relative to their structural and picturesque character.

It is well known that all travellers, native or foreign, are pleased with our city and its environs, and always call them beautiful. A stranger drives from the city through our suburban towns, winding through lanes, whose ferny and rocky sides are full of shrubs, equally beautiful with their blossoms or berries: or ascends hills that give the most varied and extended views over the bay, or far inland to the mountains; or he follows the winding course of a river, or the margin of a lake, whose clear waters give the most beautiful reflections of tree-clad banks and the changing color of the sky. Until within a few years there was no mile of the newly-annexed parts of the city destitute of special beauty of some kind; this was appreciated, and many a man to-day in other States is doing his best to adorn his grounds, or decorate the town or city in which he lives, whose love for the beautiful germinated in him when he was a boy growing up surrounded by the variety and picturesqueness of Boston's landscapes.

The best personal argument for improved public grounds is the throng of people of all ages and conditions, who fill the common, public garden, the local squares of Boston; who are counted by thousands in the Central Park of New York, and the Fairmount Park of Philadelphia, every fine day during summer. That the public want and enjoy commons and parks all admit, but what kind of a common and park they prefer is not immediately apparent; and how far it is best to try to create a correct popular taste for beauty by the character of the land selected, and its style of treatment, is also a question yet undecided. Whilst admitting that the public health requires open spaces, and that the people enjoy, and may properly have at common expense decorated grounds, many deny that Boston requires such parks and gardens as much as other cities do, because her natural advantages and beauty are so great.

There is a weak point in the argument, even if we grant its general force. Admitting that until quite lately the close suburbs of Boston were very rural and beautiful, and did give to the pedestrian, or rider, the most pleasing opportunities for exercise, and landscapes, there could be no guarantee that such chances would continue. The particular beauty of winding lane, and hedge row of brook and river bank, of lanes and avenues shaded with forest trees, the change and particular property of the village, or rural town, always fades before the growth of population, and the movement of business, as the town expands into a city.

As soon as more houses were wanted, speculators seized some fine old estate, such as that one once the glory of Roxbury, the John A. Lowell estate, and sacrificed its lawns and trees, and hedge rows to streets and tenements, wiping out beauty, and substituting therefor an ugly collection of cheap houses which deface the natural beauty of the city, as much as a smutch of black would deface and ruin a fine oil painting.

With the passage of the country place into the continuous block of bricks comes the straightening of roads, grubbing up of hedge rows, cutting down of trees, filling up of ponds and streams. Even this winter the ears of the living and the memory of the dead have been shocked by the discussion of a plan for cutting down the elms on Paddock mall; trees which remember Boston when it was a baby; trees whose sturdy trunks and branches have defied hundreds of the wildest gales, and whose natural duration of life is a thousand years, and which as scarred trunks with a few half living branches would decorate any city street, are to go, for what! The men who could cut such trees for any reason short of saving the lives of the multitudes who daily pass to and fro, thanking them for their shade in summer, and admiring their architectural beauty in winter, would readily melt the city bronzes to make bell metal, and use the city statues for foundation stones to the civic stables.

If street room is required the sidewalk may be given up, or widened, and a street made on one side of the trees, then these old giants would stand for generations to come in the turmoil and confusion and protect, as they have for generations past, the street, from sun and wind, and storm. Men maddened by the war spirit, and the fumes of sulphur and wine, tore down the great Vendome column, with its bronze statuary which was one of the honors of Paris, but the bronzes were man's work, and could be restored. Old trees can never be restored, and the names of the men who could cut them, for any but the gravest reasons, should be inscribed on a stone and sunk in the new pavement, so that their honor and glory could never be forgotten. These trees are not the only trees which have been sacrificed to city progress.

MURDERED TREES.

A very fine elm was cut last summer on the side of Warren street in Roxbury, where the new line of Harrison avenue touches that street. This elm was just becoming glorious, — its trunk was about eighteen inches in diameter and four feet girth; its branches jewelled with red buds in March and April, stretched a leafy canopy over a wide space in summer. It stood near the street and the line of the curbstone; and this tree, which could not be restored for any thousands of dollars, was cut that the line of curbstone might be uninterrupted.

Higher up on Warren street, in front of the old Warren place, another elm, about eighteen feet in circumference, which was an old tree in General Warren's childhood, was cut because, though the street is very wide there, being the junction of several streets, it would have obliged the sidewalk and the gutter to diverge from a right line.

Hundreds of most beautiful and valuable elms have been cut within a year on the new line of Stoughton street; many of them with reason; but the majority could have been saved, and trees which took a hundred years to grow, and can never be restored, because the future circumstances can never be as favorable to their growth, have gone to reappear as cord-wood on the city ledger.

The old fort on Roxbury Highlands, Cedar square, and many another piece of private and public property have, within a few years, been stripped of their fine old trees, which have sometimes been replaced by young nursery saplings, so inferior in quality and species to those they replaced that they are a sarcasm on planting and beauty. Space forbids following out each individual act of barbarism; but every street in new and old Boston, could tell its story of outrages committed or planned. Let all these facts be summoned, and as the ghastly column glides by, let us ask those who rely on Boston's natural attractions for its future park effects what may be expected. Only a tedious horse car ride will carry a poor person now where they can see any of the rural beauty of former days; it passes away and disappears before the spectator as the Indian before the white man. May's woods on Warren street, a most beautiful grove of pines, is stripped of its trees, its land cut into house lots and dug out as a quarry. Simmons' woods on the Highlands, which was most picturesque is going; wide streets have been cut through the accessible parts, huge bowlders blown into cellar stone, hill sides cut down to fill hollows. Parker's hill still exists as a hill top, thanks to the prolonged life of Mrs. Parker, but its flanks and sides are cut and gashed; huge, ugly gravel banks stare at us in place of grassy hill sides, banks which are as unimprovable and hideous as the stump of an amputated leg. Are those the places which are to be the resorts and pleasure grounds of posterity?

We easily remember what the old Fort hill in South Boston was, when as as boys we picnicked in Roxbury woods, and hunted squirrels and partridges in the meadows and pastures of West Roxbury and Dorchester, and when the granary elms were pointed out to us by our fathers as part of the leafy glories of Boston.

Then the old South Boston Fort was a great green hillside, from which we might see all the bay, the harbor, the valleys of Neponset and the Charles river. Now look at it; one visit to it with its huge bank wall of granite, its few paths, and its reservoirs, with the mind filled with old memories, will be a better homily on the wise city improvements which are to leave Boston a city of parks, than any treatise that could be written.

But it will be said that sarcasm and description of the mistakes of others are not arguments. They are the best argument, when we look at the natural advantages of Boston as she was, and partly is, and think of what the future city will be when the same treatment has been successfully applied to the more distant hills, lanes, and woodlands.

The beauty of a city, as a special feature, is as important and well worth considering by the civic authorities, as its good roads and drainage. No committee man would be willing to admit that a new city building should be made simply convenient or useful, without any regard to its effect or beauty. Plans, when presented would be analyzed, partly in relation to the good effect of the building. Why should this be, unless beauty is valuable? If it is, if buildings, statues, picture galleries, are desirable, if schools of art are to become a part of our common school system, are we to draw the line at man's creations, and neglect nature wholly? Shall we agree that nothing is good, or worth preserving, or beautiful, that is not made by contract, or devised or planned in a city office? Every summer the city fathers go somewhere for pleasure. Some seek the mountains, some the sea-side, some the quiet country farm, but wherever they go, each one proclaims in some way an appreciation of beauty. If he did not, if he openly admitted, or asserted that all he sought was the animal pleasure which comes from fruits and fresh air, fresh vegetables and country beds, he would, if not self condemned, become an object of contempt to the most of those whom he should meet. If this is true, if the beauty of the country landscape appeals to every man in different ways, let each one respect the kind of beauty he is indifferent.to, but which others admire. Let him also have charity and compassion for those whose stinted earnings give them but a small chance to seek anything outside of the city limits. Boston has many great advantages and attractions; originally built on hills, most of its streets followed the valleys, and winding through them are very picturesque even if they are inconvenient for heavy traffic. The narrow tongue of land which tied Boston to Roxbury has gradually widened into a great city; the water which used to flow over the neck in great tides is now far away, and the water basin and the water views are reduced in area. Outside of the old city limits, Roxbury, named for its rocky ledges and hill-sides covered with bowlders, was unlike any other town. There are places of equal size amongst the White and Green mountains, where the ledges and bowlders rival those of the old town of Roxbury, but they lack the little brooks that, trickling over the ledges, made them rich with mosses and lichens, the vines that climbed up their sides, the seams fringed with ferns, columbines and rosebushes, and the winding streams, whose valleys used to be the favorite haunts of the violet, aster, and gentian. The winding lanes used to lead between the rocky hills by beautiful drives to Brookline, Dedham, and Dorchester, which have the same general character of rolling country, but with less of the pudding-stone hills, whose conglomerated pebbles tell strange stories of the old pot that boiled in these regions ages ago.

From Roxbury the old roads passed through farming lands to Dorchester. Here, too, were hills and ledges, and trailing vines. The woods are going, the ledges are being buried in cellars, the lanes are straightened, and as quick as population turns a little more vigorously to the 16th ward, the hills will begin to melt before the shovel and the dirt-cart, and level lands and blocks of brick houses will take their place.

The pleasure we received from this country in the old time makes us ask are hills — is a broken, rocky landscape, — beautiful and desirable, or are these things simply a curse and hindrance to Boston, and merely a convenient source and supply of gravel and building-stone? Every cultivated person calls such natural objects beautiful in themselves, and they have additional value, because from their summits we may see combinations of beauty in the scenery forbidden to any level land, and it is plain, — self-evident, in fact, — that unless the gravest causes demand their removal they should remain. Do, in our case, any such causes exist? The first part of this treatise shows how well we can accommodate an enormous business growth without knowing any hindrance from the character of the surface, leaving us free to enjoy and utilize the beauty that the hills create and expose. If this variety and ruggedness of surface is desirable and should be preserved, as it cannot be all saved, should we preserve it in some places and let it be destroyed everywhere else?

Shall we make, for instance, one great park, locating it where we may secure the most variety, and bid all who wish to enjoy it go where it is? There are arguments in favor of such a plan. The park, with many acres of lawn and woodland, with lake and river, hill, valley and meadow, offers great opportunities for the landscape gardener's art, and permits the creation of beautiful effects which can never be produced on a small scale. No artist could resist the temptation to secure as large a tract as possible, and in most cities the weight of reason would incline us to select one great area, and decorate it in all the ways that a refined taste and imagination could suggest. But in Boston the case is not a common one. There are too many very desirable places to make it easy to select any one, and as the surface of the city is very uneven, and the space for building broken and sometimes inconvenient, a large park in one place would be apt to consume too much of the available building land, and crowd the other parts of the city with combinations of buildings not best adapted to each other.

The arguments which in many cases would be almost unanswerable for collecting all of the land for a park in a city into one large body do not at all apply to us.

To secure variety on level, or nearly level land, space is very important; but not so where every fifty acres that may be taken are broken by deep valleys, rocky hill-sides, bold ledges, ponds, or the beds of streams. Whether we take Parker's hill, the Highlands, the Williams estates, the land back of Grove Hall, or land lying near the Neponset river, we can in a comparatively small area get varieties of surface and views of the distant landscape which would make fifty acres seem larger than five times fifty of level land. This being true, we are able to do full justice to the other argument, — that parks should be dispersed through the city, so as to be accessible to all parts and divide their advantages equally among all classes of population.

Even in a level city, it may be seriously questioned whether the artistic advantages of one great park are not of less consequence than to select a number of small parks in different places, easy of access and more sure to serve as fire barriers and ventilators. But the first principle of good landscape-gardening is to adapt improvements to the natural character and features of the country or estate to be improved; and looking at a city as a great estate, and its inhabitants as a single owner, we must see that Boston, as a city, will be made more beautiful as a whole, if we can crown every hill-top with groves of trees and gardens which will have vistas opened to the landscape in addition to parks of moderate size, skirting and enclosing some of the hills and valleys which can be connected by fine avenues. These places would offer local beauty and pleasure to many neighborhoods, and to those who ride or drive, a long line of changing and beautiful scenery, each new park or common having something to admire unlike the one last passed through.

By such a system of improvements we should fix on Boston a permanent character and beauty, better, though of just the kind so much admired and recommended by those who have thought our suburbs sufficiently varied and beautiful to make special parks and pleasure-grounds of no real value to the public.

As generations pass away, the trees would grow more venerable, shrubs and flowers more dense and rich in form and color, the water would assume a more natural margin and outline, and each open area would become surrounded by fine houses with perhaps small gardens, or decorated yards, with their fronts and gables and cornices draped and festooned by the wisteria, the woodbine, roses and honeysuckles.

The buildings would harmonize with the public grounds, and shade off gradually from the park into the busy business streets. To attempt to point out how each park or common or green should be laid out, is not the part of this essay, but only to draw attention to the general theory, which must hereafter be carefully elaborated in all its details. But whilst no attempt is made to show just how the selected lands should be laid out, it is but fair to point out the different and appropriate styles of treatment which might be applied to the largest areas which are selected on the accompanying plans.

To begin with the two triangles which lie between Tremont street and Columbus avenue, bounded by Camden and Newton streets; these must be in the centre of a dense business population, and should be made to contrast strongly with their surroundings, and being in a business centre it will be most kind to those who are to work and live near by to make them shady. They should be principally planted with long-lived trees, which may, when once well established, maintain themselves for generations. But in each a space should be devoted to flowers, and perhaps a fountain; the flowers to be of the kinds which blossom longest and are most brilliant in color.

THE PROPOSED ORNAMENTAL WATER WOULD INCREASE THE WATER SUPPLY OF THE CITY.

Next comes Parker's hill, and the basin of the Back Bay. This area must always be crossed by several public roads, and one or two lines of horse cars and railroads; the largest part of the low land is now a basin of sewerage, but is the receiver of two fresh water streams, — Muddy Brook of Brookline, and Stony Brook of Roxbury. The present disposition of the city sewerage is wholly wasteful, unscientific and wrong, and the city must soon change the system of her sewerage; when that is properly taken care of these two streams will run fresh and clear, and may be dammed by the Western avenue so as to cover as much of the Back Bay as is desirable with a sheet or lake of fresh water, diversified by islands, and crossed by the great avenues on suitable bridges.

This lake, nestling under Parker's hill, would reflect its beauties, and give to one who should stand on the hill, a fine foreground for the landscape which can be seen from there. Such a lake would be a source of pleasure for old and young, summer and winter, giving a skating pond of many acres, space even for a regatta, and if well laid out and planted, with its outline broken by promontories and bays, and its surface dotted with islands, its near beauty would rival the distant views which may be seen from the hill.

Besides the beauty, the city would secure by these ponds in its centre a great reservoir of fresh water which could be sent by steam pumps to any part of the city, if desired, and thus reduce the danger which would follow an accident to the Cochituate water pipes.

Connected with this lake, by the valley of Stony Brook, above Hog's bridge, another beautiful lake and natural reservoir could be made in the valley of the Codman estate, and the chemical works.

The natural and contrasting features of Parker's hill, the Back Bay, and the valley of Stony Brook, would make a park hard to surpass in variety and beauty. No other city has as yet anything like it on the same scale.

The Fairmount Park of Philadelphia has a similar combination, but the scale is very much greater, both of hill and basin. From Parker's hill the view in all directions need only to be seen to make my language seem tame; and if the Highlands, the Codman valley, the chemical works, the Williams' estate. were all connected, divided from each other by large villages, towns in fact, but connected by a wide and well-made avenue, without consuming any huge area, we should get diversity and beauty that would satisfy the most critical person.

The Highlands, with the chemical works, Poor farm, and Codman valley, and Stony Brook dammed into a lake, would offer to the south the same general character of landscape that Parker's hill gives to the north. But what a contrast! North of Parker's hill is the city with its spires and domes, its purple lights and shadows, its bay and ships, and the distant gleam of the ocean, all to be reflected in the lake below the hill. South of the Highlands the lake would be buried in the country woods; lawns, fine residences, distant tree-clad hills, would make the landscape, and the silvery sheet of water give light and brilliancy to the whole. Now, as surely as Philadelphia could afford to take her great park to secure, improve and purify her water supply, so these two lakes would pay the city for the cost of all the lands and improvements about them.

Leaving the hills to the northwest, and following the park drive, we come to the Williams' park, which, as the plan shows, is a long and irregular piece of ground, destitute of any peculiar local character, but having many very fine forest trees, and a beautiful view over the lower harbor and bay. This park would cross Blue-hill avenue at Grove Hall, where a very pretty country opens, with rolling lands, hills and valleys, which are the source of several brooks; some parts are low and marshy, some high and ledgy, but all well adapted to park purposes, and very accessible by steam and horse cars. Here a large area could be laid out as a park for the 16th Ward and its vicinity, and the southeast side of Boston. The surface and the views are good, and a skilful landscape gardener can show what his art is able to do with good materials. The beauty of this park would be more due to the skill of man, and less to nature than the land first described. The same is true of all the land taken in Dorchester; the hill-tops have been already referred to; but any such low or level lands as may be chosen are only to be taken up and treated when they are wanted, and in such a manner as will be best able to develop a population about them. Following the line of selected land we come to the valley of the Neponset which we have already assigned reluctantly to manufacture and business; but that seems to be its destiny, though much of the valley is very hilly and cut by ravines, and evidently well adapted by its picturesque character to park-like improvements.

As we return along River street, or Boston avenue, there is a reservation between Dorchester avenue, Codman, Adams and several other streets, which should be planted and decorated when the city increases about them. Approaching the city, we come north of Meeting-house hill, to the Jones-hill park, which, as the plan shows, is only a hill with enough of the fringing low land to give easy access to to the hill, and a little variety to the surface, and to connect it with Savin hill. This high, dome-shaped hill has beautiful views and some good trees, and offers a chance for local artistic treatment, and, as is obvious, its height makes it much less desirable for building than any other land in its vicinity.

SAVIN HILL AND THE SEASHORE PARKS.

From the south side of Jones' hill we can see the interior of the city and West Roxbury, whilst from the north we may look over Dorchester, South Boston, the city and the bay. Descending this hill we come next to Savin hill, already getting thickly settled. Here, for the first time, the tourist would touch the shore of the bay, and in spite of the mud and slime deposited by our sewerage-fed harbor, the shore is beautiful, and opens out in a most attractive way. This park and its shore would be a great contrast to the others we have described, and would be a beautiful close to an afternoon's drive, which might begin and end at the Common in the city proper. From Savin hill, passing in over Boston or Dorchester avenue, the plan shows that a space has been taken on the South Bay on both sides of Dorchester brook, and the land now covered by the Norway Iron Works, where a few acres of shore and upland should be reserved and treated for the benefit of the population which must always live in that vicinity. They would at the same time that they served for their enjoyment, and as a water basin decorate this side of the South Cove, making its shores a pleasing part of the landscape from Roxbury and Harrison avenue. Winding through South Boston we reach the point that stretches out into the harbor near the Insane Asylum and the city buildings. This point, for the pleasure of South Boston, for its beauty as a part of the harbor, for its shores exposed to the harbor, ought to be reserved and knitted into our general system, and we could make a really magnificent park here. Returning to the city, let us cross the ferry to East Boston, and passing the hill tops which ought to be public property, follow the shore and the Seaside avenue out of the city limits across Breed's Island to Winthrop and Point Shirley, and return by Chelsea beach.

This drive is familiar to most of us; the heights of East Boston and Winthrop, the shore of Point Shirley, Breed's Island, and the long line of Chelsea beach, have given many a day's pleasure to old and young amongst us, and a large part of this region ought to be secured by the city for a great sea-side park for our maritime population. No matter how attractive an inland park might be, no matter how lovely its views, and hills, and ledges, and lakes, there will come days and weeks during every summer when the people yearn for the sea-shore. They fill the excursion boats to Nahant, Hull, and Hingham, to overflowing, and yet when they get to the shores they are landed on private property, and have no public or individual rights. This should not be so; if Nahant is too far away to become our sea-side park and public property, here we have at our doors a most attractive region, and a beach as beautiful as any in the country. Shall we wait until this, like Nahant, and many of our islands, have become the property of private persons, and is covered with bricks and mortar, or shall we decide now, and say, here our children and their children shall be free to roam at will, to breathe the sea air, bathe in the surf, gather shells and pebbles, and learn to love the sea, which must always be the foundation of our city's prosperity. We owe it to ourselves and to them to take care now that this part of the public domain shall be secured forever. Let Chelsea and East Boston grow more and more populous; let Charlestown and Somerville double or treble their numbers; here is the breezy sea shore, where every summer day all those who wish to come may find endless amusements and health. As we stand on the Winthrop hills, or on South Boston heights, or Savin hill, or even back on the Dorchester and Roxbury Highlands, we must recognize that the great and remarkable feature of our city is the combination of ocean, bay, harbor, islands, river, valleys and rocky headlands. Our birth and prosperity are due to these natural features; when Boston Bay was first selected for a settlement our fathers thought most of its advantageous position as a seaport for English ships; perhaps none of them had time or inclination to ascend the hills and admire the beauty of the landscape, and certainly none of them could have foreseen, even in the most richly cultivated imagination, the clustering villages, the dense city, the hundred spires, the smoking factories, the fleet of ships, which two hundred and fifty years would bring about Boston Bay.

THE PROPOSED RESERVATION SMALL FOR THE FUTURE CITY.

But even then they foresaw and imagined enough, and planned with sufficient wisdom to give to posterity a common of forty acres, which, relative to the town of Boston of that day was larger than the many acres which are comprehended in the plan which I have described. Shall we have less faith and foresight than they did? We do not need their faith, nor any exercise of imagination; for if all the public grounds I have described were appropriated and laid out, all of them would be visited by crowds the first year; and besides, we all agree, taught by experience and necessity, that such wide areas are of vital value to the life and health, independent of the pleasure of the city. We require no imagination or courage at the present day to plan wisely and greatly for Boston. If no new railroads were to come here, no new line of steamships to connect us with foreign and domestic ports, there will be by the mere natural growth of population in a hundred years so many people here, that these parks and pleasure grounds will seem as small to them as our present commons, gardens and squares do to us.

With East Boston we close our survey of the city property. In the centre of the flats on Lubec street, at least four blocks should be reserved, as also the water margin from Lubec street to where Milton street touches the water, unless Chelsea and Charlestown become part of Boston. In that case, the marginal land may be used for commerce, and the public grounds be selected in the other cities.

Having discussed the city, nothing is left of city property but the islands in the harbor.

Breed's Island is properly a part of East Boston, and could be all taken for the public to great advantage, and a part of it should be reserved, at any rate. As it is now only partly settled, the city can plan for its future with no restraint.

Breed's Island, Winthrop, and Point Shirley, ought to be parts of the city, and be bound to us by such a system of public improvements as would make them extremely desirable to live in.

The other islands, when covered with trees as our forefathers saw them, must have been most beautiful, and have given the harbor the same charming character which is the beauty of Casco Bay and of the shores of Maine. But the trees are gone, city buildings, hotels, forts, bone factories, have taken their places, and all the beauty that they retain is simply the charm that islands ever have, and the diversity they introduce into a water landscape.

All of these islands will be used in time for business purposes or dwellings; and, although one or more of them would make beautiful parks, unless they can be connected with the main land by bridges, so as to be easily and cheaply accessible to all classes of population, they ought not to be improved by the public. Some of them might be very properly taken by private enterprise for tea gardens, and so laid out and embellished as to become favorite resorts in summer.

COST NOT EXCESSIVE.

I have not discussed the cost of such a system of improvements and reservations as I have recommended, because I think its cost has nothing to do with its fitness.

Every city improvement is costly; but such of them as are actual betterments should not be feared or rejected on account of their cost.

I do not propose that the city should begin at once to condemn and remove all the existing improvements on the land to be ultimately included in this system.

In many places, as at Savin hill, along Washington street, in Roxbury, on the Parker hill reservation, the Harris and Otis places, and other similar estates and fine dwellings now standing might be left as they are, and continue to be the property of private individuals, or become sites of hospitals and public buildings.

I would encourage the growth of really handsome villages in the closest proximity, and even in the centre of some of them, so that private improvements might add their value and beauty to the grand design.

The questions of cost are as relative to the end in view as the cost of a new barn, or mill, or warehouse, is to the business man, and of no greater consequence.

If the necessity for planning for the future city is present now, or probable in the future, now is the time to think about it, and the people of the city must decide for themselves what kind of a city they will leave for their posterity. It should be no party or political question, and no clique or party should get power or place by discussing, advocating, or opposing a wise and forecasting system of public improvements. I appeal to each individual in this city to ask himself whether it is chimerical to demand that whilst we hope and plan to add to our business, our wealth and progress, that we should so arrange our territory that we can do the business we seek, and at the same time use our natural advantages with wisdom and economy. I ask every man and woman to think for themselves, whether it is likely or unlikely that their posterity will need as much breathing space, and as wide commons and squares as we do. If it is likely, calculate to-day the population to the square mile of the settled city, and the number of square feet of public grounds to the inhabitants, and say whether with the natural growth of a hundred years the proposed public grounds will be too large, and if not in a hundred, what will two hundred years demand; and it is only about two hundred years since our forefathers gave us what we have. Shall we be niggards to our children?

Because the city makes its plans for the future it does not require present increased taxation to carry out that plan; beyond the actual cost of the condemned land, and by a judicious application of the betterment law, part of the damages might be charged to those who get the direct benefit. The money required to lay out these grounds will be appropriated by posterity as they want to use them, and will be no addition to the burdens of to-day.

As this plan is read and considered, many objections must present themselves. Some persons will think it well adapted to all parts of the city but theirs; or suited to their vicinity but not to the rest; but all must admit that it is not conceived with a view to favor one part of the city, or set of land owners, more than another. I have tried to consider the city in all its parts and relations, and to give each division or portion equal future opportunities, and enable the citizens to make the most of their properties, and to judge what will be the best disposition to make when they are ready to buy, or sell, or to improve any particular piece of ground. That my plan will seem to many extravagant, to some injudicious or crude, I expect. But it may turn the public thought to the subject and help the formation of a sound opinion, which will open into a well digested and perfectly satisfactory plan, which, when it is executed, will not only enable Boston to do an immense business satisfactorily and with economy, but make the city beautiful in all its parts, and an honor to the country.

ROBERT MORRIS COPELAND.